I LOVE TO HELP
MI PIACE AIUTARE

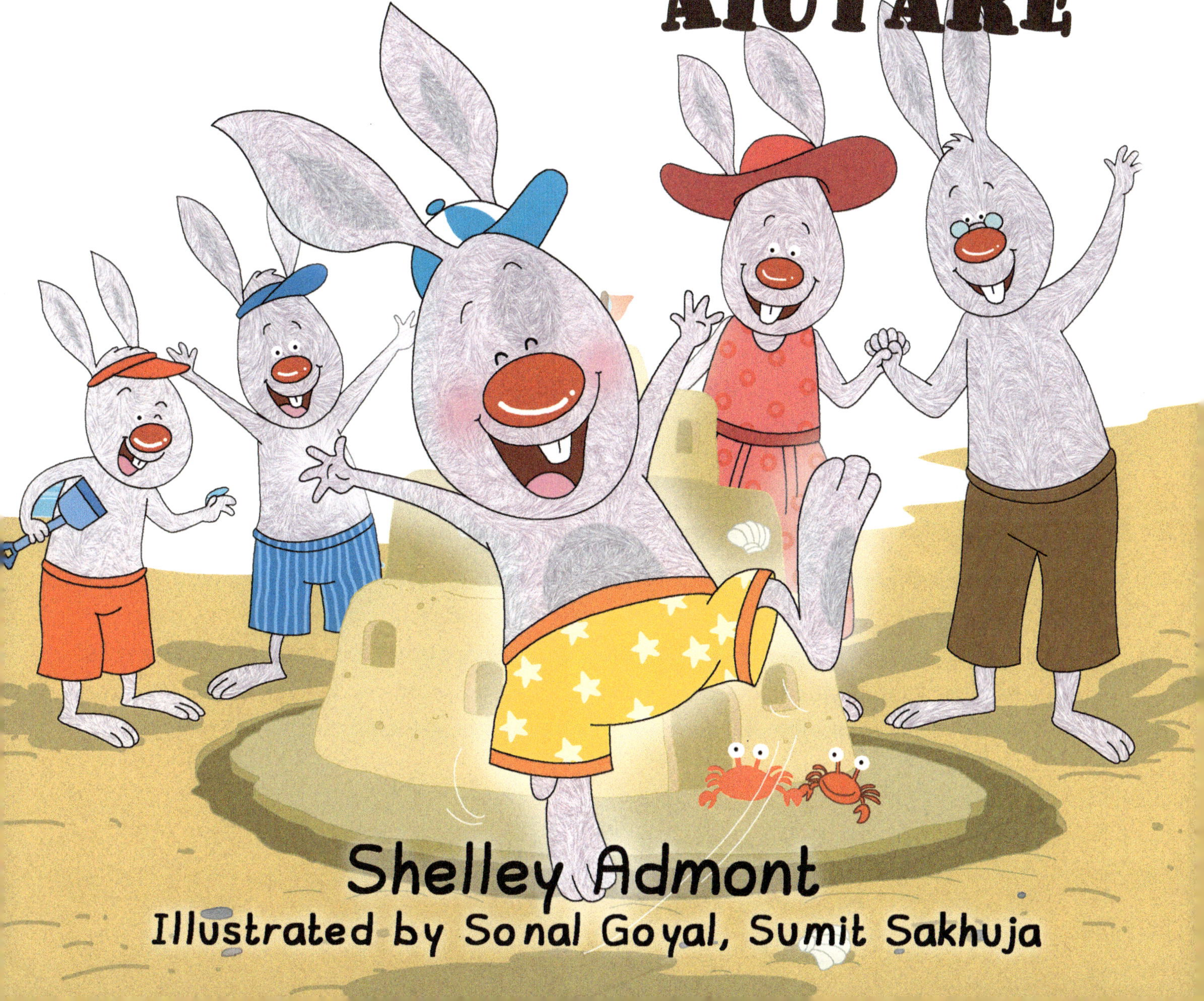

Shelley Admont
Illustrated by Sonal Goyal, Sumit Sakhuja

www.sachildrensbooks.com

Copyright©2016 by S. A. Publishing

innans@gmail.com

All rights reserved. No part of this book may be reproduced in any form or by any electronic or mechanical means, including information storage and retrieval systems, without written permission from the publisher or author, except in the case of a reviewer, who may quote brief passages embodied in critical articles or in a review.

Tutti i diritti sono riservati. Nessuna parte di questa pubblicazione può essere riprodotta, memorizzata in sistemi di recupero o trasmessa in qualsiasi forma o attraverso qualsiasi mezzo elettronico, meccanico, mediante fotocopiatura, registrazione o altro, senza l'autorizzazione del possessore del copyright.

First edition, 2016

Translated from English by Anna Cortese

Traduzione dall'inglese a cura di Anna Cortese

Library and Archives Canada Cataloguing in Publication

I Love to Help (Italian Bilingual Edition)/ Shelley Admont

ISBN: 978-1-77268-867-2 paperback

ISBN: 978-1-77268-868-9 hardcover

ISBN: 978-1-77268-866-5 eBook

Please note that the Italian and English versions of the story have been written to be as close as possible. However, in some cases they differ in order to accommodate nuances and fluidity of each language.

Although the author and the publisher have made every effort to ensure the accuracy and completeness of information contained in this book, we assume no responsibility for errors, inaccuracies, omission, inconsistency, or consequences from such information.

For those I love the most-S.A.
Per quelli che amo di pi -S.A.

Jimmy bounced around the car in excitement.
Jimmy saltellava intorno alla macchina, tutto emozionato.

"We're going to the beach!" he shouted happily. "We're going to the beach!"
"Andiamo al mare!" gridò felice. "Andiamo al mare!"

Dad laughed as he opened the trunk of the car. "That's right!" he said, "It's a lovely sunny day and we want to get going quickly."
Il papà rise, aprendo il portellone posteriore dell'auto. "Esatto!" disse, "E' una splendida giornata di sole e vogliamo partire al più presto."

"Why don't you help us carry the things we need to the car? Your brothers are helping already."
"Perché non ci aiuti a trasportare l'occorrente in macchina? I tuoi fratelli ci stanno già aiutando."

Jimmy stopped bouncing and looked towards the front door of their house.

Jimmy smise di saltellare e guardò verso il portone d'ingresso della loro casa.

Jimmy's two brothers were helping carry things to the car.

I suoi due fratelli stavano aiutando a portare il necessario alla macchina.

The oldest brother had colorful buckets and spades in his hands, and the middle brother was carrying the picnic basket.

Il fratello maggiore aveva tra le mani secchielli colorati e palette, mentre il fratello di mezzo stava trasportando il cestino da picnic.

"Come, Jimmy!" Mom called from the doorway. "You can carry the bag of towels or this small beach chair. It won't be very hard."

"Vieni, Jimmy!" lo chiamò la mamma dall'ingresso. "Tu puoi portare la sacca dei teli mare o questa piccolo sdraio. Non dovrebbe essere troppo faticoso."

Jimmy looked at the towels and chair. "No, thank you!" he said with a grin. "I'm too busy JUMPING!"

Jimmy lanciò uno sguardo ai teli mare e allo sdraio. "No, grazie!" disse con un largo sorriso. "Sono troppo impegnato a SALTELLARE!"

The forest where they lived was not too far from the beach and Jimmy wriggled with excitement the whole way.

Il bosco dove vivevano non era distante dalla spiaggia e Jimmy si dimenò emozionato per tutto il viaggio.

When he saw the golden sands of the beach and the sparkling blue water of the sea, he started jumping in his seat.

Quando vide la sabbia dorata della spiaggia e la luccicante acqua azzurra del mare, cominciò a saltellare sul suo sedile.

"Alright, we are here," said Dad. "Let's get out and enjoy the day!"

"Eccoci arrivati!" disse il papà. "Usciamo e godiamoci la giornata!"

Jimmy got out of the car. "This is amazing," he exclaimed and ran down towards the water.

Jimmy scese dall'auto. "E' fantastico!" esclamò e corse giù, verso l'acqua.

"Wait!" Mom called after him. "You've got to help us to take everything out of the car."

"Aspetta!" lo chiamò la mamma. "Devi aiutarci a scaricare tutto dalla macchina."

Jimmy turned around, waving at his family. "No, thank you!" he said. "I've got to build a GIANT SANDCASTLE!"

Jimmy si girò, salutando con la mano la sua famiglia. "No, grazie!" disse. "Devo costruire un GIGANTESCO CASTELLO DI SABBIA!"

He ran to a perfect spot on the beach, right next to the sea, and started to scoop sand into his hands.

Corse verso un luogo adatto sulla spiaggia, proprio di fianco al mare, e cominciò a scavare nella sabbia con le mani.

Jimmy was so busy having fun that he didn't notice his family going to and from the car, carrying objects down to the beach.

Jimmy era così impegnato da non accorgersi che la sua famiglia stava facendo avanti e indietro dalla macchina, trasportando vari oggetti in spiaggia.

Meanwhile, the sandcastle grew bigger and bigger.

Nel frattempo, il castello di sabbia diventava sempre più grande.

Jimmy used the buckets to build towers, made a great wall of sand joining them and even started digging a moat around the outside to keep the castle safe.

Jimmy usò i secchielli per costruire le torri, fece un alto muro di sabbia per unirle e cominciò perfino a scavare un fossato tutto intorno, per tenere il castello al sicuro.

"My castle is going to be so big, a King and Queen are going to want to move in!" Jimmy said, imagining tiny knights and servants running around inside.

"Il mio castello sarà così grande che un Re e una Regina vorranno venire ad abitarci!" disse Jimmy, immaginando piccoli cavalieri e servitori correre al suo interno.

While Jimmy was working on his castle, his older brothers were hunting for the biggest shell they could find.

Mentre Jimmy stava lavorando al suo castello, i suoi fratelli maggiori andarono a caccia della più grande conchiglia che potessero trovare.

Dad went swimming in the sea, looking at the fish with his snorkel, and Mom lay on a towel further up the beach.

Il papà andò a nuotare in mare e la mamma si distese su un telo mare distante, sulla spiaggia.

Jimmy was so focused on his castle that he didn't really notice what the rest of his family were doing until...

Jimmy era così concentrato sul suo castello da non accorgersi di che cosa stesse facendo il resto della sua famiglia finché...

"Watch out!" Jimmy heard his dad shout.

"Attento!" Jimmy sentì gridare dal papà.

He looked up just in time to see a giant wave rising up beside him from the sea!

Guardò in su, giusto in tempo per vedere un'onda gigantesca avvicinarsi dietro di lui dal mare!

"Oh no!" cried Jimmy as the wave crashed down on top of him. When the water pulled away, Jimmy lay on his back and tried to catch his breath.

"Oh no!" gridò Jimmy quando l'onda si abbatté su di lui. Quando l'acqua si ritirò, Jimmy si distese a pancia in su, e provò a riprendere fiato.

"Yuck!" Jimmy spat out salty water and pulled seaweed from behind his ears.

"Puah!" Jimmy sputacchiò acqua salata e si tolse un'alga da dietro l'orecchio.

Then he looked up to see what had happened to his castle.

Poi guardò in su per vedere cosa fosse successo al suo castello.

"Noooo!" he cried. The castle was completely destroyed!

"Noooo!" gridò. Il castello era completamente distrutto!

Jimmy felt hot tears on his face as he looked at the ruined castle.

Jimmy sentì calde lacrime scorrere sul suo viso mentre osservava le rovine del castello.

Mom knelt down beside him and gave him a hug. All his family had stopped what they were doing and gathered around him.

La mamma si inginocchiò al suo fianco e lo abbracciò. Tutta la sua famiglia aveva smesso di fare quello che stava facendo e si era riunita attorno a lui.

"I'm sorry about your castle," Dad said.
"Mi dispiace per il tuo castello," disse il papà.

"Yeah, it looked really cool," said the oldest brother.
"Già, era davvero bello," disse il fratello maggiore.

"And big," agreed the middle brother.
"E grande," concordò il fratello di mezzo.

Mom smiled. "Don't worry, Jimmy. We'll help you build a new one."
La mamma sorrise.
"Non ti preoccupare, Jimmy. Ti aiuteremo a costruirne uno nuovo."

"You will?" Jimmy asked.
"Lo farete davvero?" chiese Jimmy.

"Yes!" His family laughed and they all set about building the sandcastle again.
"Certo!" La sua famiglia rise e si misero tutti insieme a costruire di nuovo il castello di sabbia.

Something was different this time. Jimmy realized that with his family helping him, the castle was bigger and more beautiful than before.

Ma questa volta c'era qualcosa di diverso. Jimmy realizzò che con l'aiuto della sua famiglia, il castello era più grande e più bello di prima.

"Look!" the oldest brother pointed inside. Two crabs had settled down in the center of the castle. "It even has a King and Queen!"

"Guardate!" disse il fratello più grande indicando l'interno. Due granchi si erano sistemati al centro del castello. "Ha perfino un Re e una Regina!"

Jimmy bounced up and down. "This is the best sandcastle ever!"

Jimmy saltellò su e giù. Questo è il più bel castello di sempre!"

When it was time to go, the family began taking things back into the car.

Quando fu il momento di andare, la famiglia cominciò a riportare indietro gli oggetti alla macchina.

Jimmy grinned. "May I help you?" he asked.

Jimmy fece un grande sorriso. "Posso aiutarvi?" chiese.

He took the towels to the car and then ran back to help carry the buckets and spades too.

Portò i teli mare alla macchina, poi tornò indietro per aiutare a trasportare i secchielli e perfino le palette.

"Wow, we packed that really quickly," Dad said when they were done, looking at the empty beach.

"Wow, l'abbiamo caricato davvero in un baleno," disse il papà quando ebbero finito, guardando verso la spiaggia vuota.

Even when they came home, Jimmy continued to help, carrying the beach chairs back into the house.

Anche quando tornarono a casa, Jimmy continuò ad aiutare, trasportando le sdraio in casa.

"Everything works out better when we help each other," he told Mom.

"Tutto funziona meglio quando ci aiutiamo l'un l'altro," disse alla mamma.

Mom smiled. "Well, the car is empty now, except for one thing."

La mamma sorrise. "Bene, ora la macchina è vuota, eccetto per una cosa."

Mom pulled out a packet of cookies. "I think someone needs to help eat these cookies!"

La mamma tirò fuori un sacchetto di biscotti. "Penso che qualcuno mi debba aiutare a mangiare questi biscotti!"

Jimmy laughed. "Yes, please! I'll help."

Jimmy rise. "Sì, per favore! Lo faccio io."

Lightning Source UK Ltd.
Milton Keynes UK
UKOW07f0206071216
289380UK00006B/31/P

9 781772 688672